# Rain Forest Homes

Lydia Carlin

SCHOLASTIC INC.

NEW YORK • TORONTO • LONDON • AUCKLAND • SYDNEY
MEXICO CITY • NEW DELHI • HONG KONG • BUENOS AIRES

ISBN-13: 978-0-545-00717-7 / ISBN-10: 0-545-00717-8

Photos Credits:
Cover: © Kevin Schafer/Corbis; title page: © Bob Krist/Corbis; contents page, from top: © Frans Lanting/Minden Pictures, © Michael& Patricia Fogden/Minden Pictures, © Mark Moffett/Minden Picture; page 4: © Frans Lanting/Minden Pictures; page 5, top: © Frans Lanting/Minden Pictures; page 5, bottom: © George Bernard/Animals Animals; page 6, top: © Luiz Claudio Marigo/Nature Picture Library; page 6, bottom: © Tom Vezo/Nature Picture Library; page 7, top: © Michael & Patricia Fogden/Minden Pictures; page 7, bottom: © Premaphotos/Nature Picture Library; page 8: © Michael & Patricia Fogden/Minden Pictures; page 8, inset: © Ingo Arndt/Foto Natura/Minden Pictures; page 9: © Stuart Westmorland/Getty Images; page 10: © Frans Lanting/Minden Pictures; page 11, top and bottom: © Frans Lanting/Minden Pictures; page 12: © Mark Moffett/Minden Picture; page 13: © Martin Harvey/Foto Natura/Minden Pictures; page 13, inset: © Pete Oxford/Nature Picture Library; page 14: © Claus Meyer/Minden Pictures; page 14, inset: © RF/Corbis; page 15: © Gunther Michael/Bios/Peter Arnold Inc.; page 15, inset: © Richard Du Toit/Nature Picture Library; page 16: © Frans Lanting/Minden Pictures; back cover: © Mark Payne-Gill/Nature Picture Library.

Photo research by Dwayne Howard
Design by Holly Grundon



12 11 10 9 8 7 6 5 4 3 8 9 10 11 12/0

Printed in the U.S.A.
First printing, September 2007

# Contents

## Chapter 1

# In the Rain Forest

Welcome to the rain forest! Rain forests are warm and **humid**. Rain falls almost every day.

**Scarlet macaws live in the trees.**

**Jaguars live on the ground.**

All the rain causes lots of plants to grow. The plants make rain forests a great home for animals.

**Fast Fact**

**Sadly, people are cutting down many of the trees in the world's rain forests.**

**morpho butterfly**

**eyelash viper**

Blue! Yellow! Red! Green! The rain forest is filled with creatures of every color.

**strawberry poison dart frog**

**green shield bug**

**Fast Fact**

**Animals like these will disappear if the world's rain forests disappear.**

Flutter! Slither! Hop! Creep! More animals live here than any other place on Earth.

Chapter 2

# Homes in the Trees

Trees in the rain forest are alive with life! Sloths live in trees. They snooze about 15 hours a day. Zzzzzz!

Toucans live in trees. They use their bright beaks to pick fruit. Did you know they can croak like frogs?

Orangutans live in trees. They use their long, strong arms to swing from branch to branch.

A green chameleon is happy.

A gray chameleon is cold.

**Chameleons** (kuh-**mee**-lee-uhnz) live in trees. These funny-looking lizards can change colors.

Chapter 3

# Homes on the Ground

The ground of the rain forest is crawling with creatures! Leafcutter ants live on the ground. They **cart** leaves back to their nests all day long.

**Tapirs** (**tay**-purz) live on the ground. These shy mammals eat grass, leaves, and fruit. Munch, munch, munch!

Fast Fact

**Anacondas are the world's biggest snakes. Some are as long as a school bus.**

**Anacondas** live on the ground. During the day, they keep cool in **swamps**. At night, they slither out to hunt for food. Ssssss!

**Fast Fact**

**The rhinoceros beetle is named after the rhinoceros. Do you think they look alike?**

Rhinoceros beetles live on the ground. They are just one of the amazing animals that call the rain forest home sweet home!

# Glossary

**anaconda** (an-uh-**kon**-duh): a large snake that lives in the rain forests of South America

**cart** (**kart**): to carry

**chameleon** (kuh-**mee**-lee-uhn): a type of lizard that can change color

**humid** (**hyoo**-mid): damp and moist

**swamp** (**swahmp**): an area of wet, spongy ground

**tapir** (**tay**-pur): a large animal with hooves and a long snout

## Comprehension Questions

1. Can you tell about one animal that lives in the trees of the rain forest?
2. Can you tell about one animal that lives on the ground of the rain forest?
3. Can you think of three great words to describe a rain forest?